A LETTER FROM PONTUS
AND OTHER VERSE

A LETTER FROM PONTUS

AND OTHER VERSE

By John Masefield

New York

THE MACMILLAN COMPANY

1 9 3 6

FIRST PRINTING

PRINTED IN THE UNITED STATES OF AMERICA
BY THE STRATFORD PRESS, INC., NEW YORK

TO
MY WIFE

Contents

A LETTER FROM PONTUS
AND OTHER VERSE

A Letter from Pontus

In the first year of the Divine Tiberius,
I went as junior on a Legate's staff
To view the Danube frontier and report.
After a summer on the river there,
I was despatched to Tomi, on the Euxine,
To winter, and to learn what could be done
To keep the savages from pillaging,
With orders to proceed to Rome in Spring
By the first ship, when sailing recommenced.

I wintered in that horrible black den
And learned, beyond all doubt, what should be done
To bitt the bridle on those savages;
And had the privilege besides to lodge
With Ovid, the great poet, exiled there.

He was unlike the Ovid in my mind,
(All graceful, wanton, charming, credulous,)
Being an old, bleak, broken-hearted man
Dressed in wool trowsers and a sheepskin coat,
Living in dire poverty on biscuit,
Salt mullet and the country vinegar.
He had a one-roomed hovel, floored with clay,
A lamp, a bed of goatskins, a few books,
A hearth, where seldom any firing burned,
A few fair relics of his happiness,
And implements for writing: nothing else.

I

I did not know his people, nor he mine;
But being from the City I was welcome
To him, so long removed from anyone
Or any thing, that made him happy once.
He made me share his little through the winter,
And little though it was I should have fared
Hardly, without it, in that frontier town,
Ringed by the barrens blackened by east wind.
Later, the snow fell, and the frost set in,
A silent, intense cold, night after night,
With starved birds dead upon the snow next day.
Mad savages, half starved, on starving ponies,
Came raiding down and shot their poisoned arrows
Over our crazy walls at us, and screamed.
It was more madman's nightmare than a life.
But always Ovid as a charming host
Cheered and distracted and delighted me
Through all those months, not speaking of himself,
But giving me the wonders of his mind.
He said he had not talked for seven years.
And what was trebly precious, he insisted
On writing my Report; imagine it,
A subaltern's Report upon the Getae
Written by the most famous living poet.
I was promoted for it the next year.

I never met a mind so full of grain:—
Other men's grain perhaps, but there it was

A wealth of knowledge, which came flashing out
From some old world of beauty and romance
To make to-day's occasions beautiful.
He had been famous, as men said, since childhood,
For touching powers of reciting verse.
Towards the ending of the winter time
He sometimes spoke for me; pathetic tales,
Old ballads which had charmed him as a boy,
Messenger speeches from forgotten plays;
All spoken with a golden tenderness
Which broke the hearts of those rough listeners
(For many begged to listen when he spoke).
They had been puzzled by him there at first
And often thwarted and insulted him.
But he had won them; he was privileged
To pay no taxes as a citizen,
(No little mercy in a town so poor)
And people stared at him as he went by
And muttered "That's the man Augustus feared . . . .
He cuckolded the Cæsar, so they say."

So winter wore away and floods began;
Then, lo, as they subsided presently,
One sunset, there was cheering from the tower
And people cried "The ship from Athens signalled,
Summer is here: sailing has recommenced."

Next morning, when she entered into port,
Most of us went to watch her: Ovid stayed.

He had been disappointed, spring by spring,
Of pardon, or recall, or messages
From those he loved; he now expected nothing;
Nor was there anything for him to-day.
But letters and delightful things from Rome
Were there for me, as olives, anchovies,
And comfort from our vineyard of black grapes,
With orders from my chiefs beside for me
To take that ship when she returned for Corinth
Just one week later, seven days from then.

I counted every hour of those days.
Could the time pass? Would nothing intervene
To keep me prisoned in that cursed den?
Suppose the ship should perish in the harbour,
Or I fall sick and be refused aboard?
Yet with this horror of anxiety
I had some grace of horror for poor Ovid.
He had been charming to me utterly;
Now I was going to the City, home
To Italy, the summer sea and sunshine,
To friends and lovely women and delight,
While he would stay alone in Tomi there
All summer, with a winter at the end
Like that just passed, and never any hope
Of mercy or forgiveness or release,
As someone killed and buried and forgotten.

The night before the morning of the sailing,
He said to me "You often longed to ask
Why I was exiled here, but ever feared
To hurt my feelings. When you sail to-morrow,
Carry this letter with you, back to Rome,
Bear it at sunset to the Pincian Hill
And read it there, surveying the world's Queen,
And think of me in Tomi, on the Euxine.
It tells my story. Will you do this for me?"

The sun was shining as we walked together
To where the ship lay at the watering-pier.
There is a shrub, like almond, with pink blossom,
Most common in that country in the spring;
Our way led through a meadow of it then,
Full flowered, full of honey, loud with bees.
Below, the ship lay at her watering-place.
Beyond her, trembled the blue way to freedom.

The poet stopped above the jetty-end:
"I will not follow to the pier," he said;
"We'll say farewell: God prosper you, my son.
May your report delight your generals
And bring you the promotions you would choose."
So, there we parted, and I went aboard.
I saw him as we sailed still standing there,
Not moving, staring at the something free
That bore a luckier exile back to Rome.

He had not stirred when we lost sight of him.
I think he may have stood there all day long.

Many bright billows, many shadowy mountains,
And sea be-battered islands spouting spray
Lie between Pontus and the Pincian Hill.

This is the letter which the poet gave me.
I read it in the gardens, looking west
At sunset on the city as he bade.

"Fortune is intermingled with disaster,
Glory with ruin, triumph with decay,
My downfall had its roots in my success.

Two roots:—a book of verses about Love,
Which made me the delight of gallant Rome;
And Julia, the Cæsar's grand-daughter,
Fed my disastrous harvest of despair.
She was the princess of that glittering world.
She flattered me to help her in preparing
A play, with choral odes, for Roman nobles
To sing to Cæsar's self upon his birthday.

My play, *Medea,* was the chosen work.
I wrote the choral odes in a few days.
All the young nobles who could act or sing
(Some thirty, no bad harvest from such soil)
Gathered together in the happy scheme,
Day after day within the Pauline palace,

6

Under myself, the poet of light love,
And Julia, the goddess of the same.

Julia was bright damnation to the young.
Greedy, as one consumptive, lovely, reckless,
Fevered, clutching at youth now swiftly fading,
Hating her grandfather, the Cæsar's self,
Hating (and mocking, too,) the Cæsar's wife.
But she was beautiful unthinkably.
Her little, clear, adorable bright head
So neat, so exquisite . . . I told her once
"Ah, had I been a generation younger
And bred a sculptor, not a poet, Julia,
I would have wrought an image of that head
(That little, neat, impeccable, bright head
So exquisitely poised upon its neck)
With so much ecstasy of adoration
That the hard marble would have turned to flesh
As happened to the Greek."
                                        I think it pleased her.

She had little, hot, thin hands, and haggard eyes
Bright as two stars, restless as serpent's tongues,
She had her mother's wit, her father's courage.
Her brown hair, banded close about her head,
Shewed the skull's beauty and kept hidden from us
Her one defect, her ears. I saw them once.

I have a rule I never yet knew fail.
Damnable women have ignoble ears.
Beautiful ears are rarer than good verse.
Her ears were a malefic mark upon her.
I saw them; but too late to take the warning.

What happy days in that great rambling palace,
Filled with the relics and the memories
Of two most noble families of men,
Whose images and swords and oak leaf crowns
Were with us as we sang and acted there.
The choruses of young men sang my words
To flutes and strings: my tragic scene was tried:
We were as merry as the grasshoppers,
Laughing and singing all day long together,
Then feasting on the stage, re-telling gaily
The merry moments of the day just passed.

Yet, as the days passed, it was clear to me
That those bright haggard eyes were after prey;
They were intent upon the gallant lad
Who acted Jason and sang bass in the ode.
Coming too early to the stage one morning,
I saw them; beyond doubt they were two lovers.
I tiptoed back, unheard, no spoil-sport, I.
I, who had taught the art, could not blame pupils
Yet the outrageous boldness startled me . . .

8

There, in her husband's house, the Emperor's grand-
    child,
What madness and what danger, yet what fun.

"This, then," I thought, "explains her sudden zeal,
For poetry and singing and Augustus,
All three become her pandars to her love."

Alas; there was another explanation.

There was a feud then among Cæsar's Kin
Which, of two claimants, should succeed Augustus:—
Tiberius, the step-son, or the grand-son,
Agrippa Postumus, his daughter's child.
The Empress plotted for her son Tiberius;
But we, who did not love the Cæsaress,
Loved him still less, that secret with slow jaws
Which mumbled twenty years but bit at last.
Julia, the reckless, plotted for Agrippa,
He was her brother and the rightful heir.
But I, who did not love Tiberius,
Could not support Agrippa's claim to rule,
He was a boy, a sullen, vengeful boy
Not rightly sane, but strong as Heracles.
Beautiful, yes, but often moody-mad.
Cæsar, who reckoned him unfit to rule,
Had sent him to his island, long before.

As Destiny decided, so it fell.

9

One midnight, when our company dispersed,
I recollected, as I hurried home,
That (for the first time since our party formed)
I had not timed the meeting for next day.
I thought, "I'll hurry back, and catch them there,
(They will not all have gone) and name a time."

An instant's instinct said, "I will go home,
And send them word by messenger, to-morrow."
Then "No," I muttered, "It is but five minutes . . .
Five minutes walk by moonlight . . . I'll go back."

I recollect so well the very place
Where my unhappy Fortune bade me turn.
A little square from which three alleys led.
Within the centre, dolphins spouted water
Into a marble bowl with gleam and splash.
There was a temple doorway with a lantern;
Its light gleamed on the helmet of a guard
Who stood, with grounded spear, watching all passers.

I turned beside the fountain to my death.

The servant at the postern let me in,
With word that some of my companions lingered.
Though all the palace household seemed asleep,
I stumbled down deserted corridors
Until I saw our meeting-room ahead
Peopled, it seemed, well-lit, the door ajar.

Then, as I hurried to the lighted space,
I heard the clear voice of our Julia's lover,
Saying, "So friends, we are agreed together?
We shall attempt no cutting short of Cæsar
By one least minute; but when Cæsar dies,
The Empress and Tiberius shall fall,
We'll have Agrippa Postumus as Cæsar."
"We will," the voices cried. Then my foot tripped
They had a cord across the corridor.
"Who's there?" one called. There was no drawing back.
I answered, "Ovid"; then, as I recovered,
The truth was certain to me as though told . . .
Cæsar had been unwell some little time . . . .
These, taking all their hopes as facts, expected
That he would die and now were plotting there
To make Agrippa Postumus the Cæsar
In name, while Julia and her lover ruled.
This was the explanation of her zeal
For Ovid's poems and Augustus' birthday.

I entered in, to a scared company.

Julia, her lover, and nine singers stood there
Knowing that I had overheard their treason.
Eleven pairs of eyes were fixed on me.

There were two singers whom I much disliked,
One red, the other dun, both faced with masks,
Two wooden faces, yet with steely eyes.

I knew that both had thoughts of killing me,
I saw the same thought passing in their minds:
"Silence this interloper here and now,
And leave his body in the lane below;
The people finding it will say: "Poor Ovid,
Murdered by footpads going home last night."
I was in danger for a little instant.

"Ah, gentlemen," I cried, "You must not fear me.
"I'll not betray you; follow your device.
What I have overheard is safe from me . . .
We are old friends."

       I saw the killers' eyes
Turn towards Julia for confirmation.
She, who was watching me, laughed quietly.
"Of course," she said, "we are old, proven friends."
"Of course," the younger of the killers echoed,
"We have no fear."
       "No," said the elder killer,
"That goes without our saying: none at all."
"Truly," I said, "Here is my hand upon it."

We all shook hands upon my trustiness.
"My friends," I said, "I am fast growing old,
And prudence is the penalty of age.
But might I, as an old friend, counsel prudence?
A closed door and a sentinel outside?

Suppose I had not been the poet Ovid,
No, but a prose-writer, or Cæsar's spy,
(Such things exist) what ruin to the ode,
What tragedy within a tragedy.
At least be prudent till our play is done."

So, with uneasiness and laughter mixed,
We chatted for a little, then dispersed;
One, whom I cherished most of all the singers,
Asked to walk home with me: I granted leave,
Though qualms were in me as we started forth,
Lest he should be the comrade picked to kill
A doubtful member of the brotherhood.
Who can be safe among conspirators?
When we were clear of all the company,
In the bright moonlight, safe from any spy,
He said "This folly of conspiracy,
Mad in design and reckless in procedure,
Will end in ruin as I ever feared.
Your coming in to night has ended me
As one of such a crazy company.
No more such risk for me: to-morrow morning,
I shall exchange into the Spanish Legion
And start away at once for further Spain."

He kept his word: we never saw him more.
His place was taken by another singer.

Then, three days later, one among us called me
Aside into a passage in the palace,
To a still corner up above some stairs;
(Dark-railed the stairs, the walls were speckled marble.
I am unlikely to forget the place.)
He said, "You know the singer we call Shock-head?"
"Shock-head" was chief of those I called the killers.
I answered "Yes, of course, what of him, then?"
"Why, this," he said, "He has not come to sing
These two rehearsals; he is not at home,
Nor at his daily pleasures in the city.
Thinking he might be at his country place,
I asked his parents; but he is not there.
Ovid, I know from someone whom I trust,
That he is in the palace of Augustus.
He and his comrade both are Cæsar's spies.
You have not anything to fear, of course,
But I, O heaven, Ovid, I was mad
To join this crazy venture; I am going
Now, at this very instant, where I can."
Then with some broken words he shook my hand
And slipping down the stairway disappeared.

The next day Julia's lover whispered to me
"Ovid, it might be prudent to leave Rome."

Thinking the warning good I went from Rome,
With some misgivings for my friends perhaps,

Not any for myself: I saw the sea,
Enjoyed the sun, made verses, tasted wines
From famous little vineyards: a week passed.

Then suddenly the dearest friend I have
Came post to find me, bringing dreadful news:—
"The Lady Julia is in arrest,
With young Silanus, said to be her lover.
A dozen others are in jeopardy,
For plotting for the mad Agrippa boy;
The rumour is, that you are in it, too.
For God's sake, brother, say it isn't true."

The lightning of my danger flashed upon me.
I stood like someone stricken to the death
Uncertain how to fall; he read my face;
I saw that he had read it; then he said
"O hurry back to Rome and shew yourself.
Your absence in itself causes suspicion,
My horses are at door: return with me."

Within one hour of my reaching home,
An officer of the Imperial Guard
Bade me attend the palace on the morrow.
I asked, for what; he said he did not know,
But thought that Cæsar wished to speak to me
Concerning gallant verses about love.

* * *

There was wreathed laurel on Augustus' door.
I was admitted to the waiting-room.
There were some officers from Germany
Who brought despatches and some German weapons
(Heavy, long, thrusting spears) to shew to Cæsar;
The captain called them to the presence soon
And I was left alone, counting the streaks
In the cold marble while my heart misgave
And officers and clerks passed to and fro.
I waited while the morning wore away.
Then from without, an officer, cried "Guard,
Turn out. Fall in. Attention. Present arms."
And someone shuffled panting in the passage.
He shuffled in at length; a ghastly man,
Legatus once in farther Syria,
Shaking, and dying, from a fever-fit,
His starting eyes already glazed with death
Yet having to report before he died.
He watched me with the speechless interest
Which dying men display in living men,
But did not speak: a long long time we sat there.
At last with chattering teeth and huddled cloak,
He moved (half carried) into Cæsar's presence,
While I remained, recalling scraps of verse,
Watching the patterns painted on the walls,
And dreading now what Cæsar had to say.

After a time, a captain of the guard
Led me into another room and said

"Wait here a little: I expect the Chief
Will see you soon. The weapons in the stands
Were brought from Gaul by Divine Julius
Whose statue there awaits a verse from you."

I wondered if the Cæsar wanted verses,
Verses from me about that first of Cæsars,
That killer of the commonwealth of Rome,
Murdered upon our murdered liberties,
Whose brazen ruthless face was posted there.
Such happy fortune was not to be mine.

Suddenly I was summoned in to Cæsar.
He sat beneath a window so that light
Blazed full upon my face and dazzled me;
I scarcely saw him, but saluted him.
He was "Divine Augustus," even then.
Divinity of Fortune and of Place
Made him inhuman, liker god than man.
And what of all the godhead did I see
There in the whiteness of that sunny room?
I saw a little purple and some gold
A chair of bronze, a white robe, a white head
Which swayed the world a thousand miles away,
Turn where you would; a little cold white voice
Spoke to me without passion, finally.

"I have been looking at your Book of Love.
I need not tell the danger of such books

To all the many thoughtless of the young.
Nor need I warn you that its teaching runs
Counter to recent policies and acts
Not lightly framed and all too necessary.
It is no little matter to the State
When genius is linked with the disruptive.

And latterly you have allied yourself
With scholars of the teachings you profess.
Adultery and household treachery,
In this case added to conspiracy.

As an acquaintance of my daughter's child,
Your life and property, though confiscate,
Will both be spared; yourself will have one month
To settle your affairs and say farewell;
Then, on word given, you will go to Tomi,
In Pontus, or the Euxine, and there stay.
Fame says it is the city where Medea
Killed and cut up her brother."

                        His hand fell.
A captain of his body-guard was there
To help my stunned self, blinded from the god,
Out of the presence to my misery.
That is the story of the fall of Ovid.

This is the eighth year of my banishment.
Little remains to tell and none to tell to.

I wrote *Medea* in the savage tongue
And taught the savages to play the piece
With choral odes. I used to hope at first.
My miseries compelled me to beseech,
Beg, supplicate, with abject flatteries,
Whining for mercy. That is over now;
For I shall perish and be buried here.
After the summer season comes the winter.
I had the sunny city in my youth,
More happiness, more charming friends, more fame,
Than fell to any poet of the time.

It may be that the miseries of men
Fulfil some purpose of the deities
For each man's spirit on its pilgrimage.
I who have tasted both of life's extremes,
Who used to pray for never-ending life,
That so I might survey the field of fable,
Of men and gods immingled, interchanged,
In the bright light that only poets see
And bring into sweet verse the truths perceived,
Thinking eternity too short a time
For so much glory, were the power granted,
Now ask for nothing, save perhaps to help
What misery I can, with what I have,
Before an everlasting peace of death."

This is the letter which the poet gave me.
I read it there upon the Pincian Hill,

Weeping for that old broken-hearted host
So soon to die among the savages,
Far from the lovely women who had loved him.
Years later, an old lady sent for me,
One of the greatest ladies then in Rome.
She asked me much of Ovid as I knew him,
And wept to hear, and blessed me for my caring.
She said "I was the one he called Corinna,
When Life was April and between us two."

Australia

When the North Lander saw the rose in blossom,
He thought the bush bore fire, and knelt and prayed.
When first the desert woman saw the sea,
She cried, "O under God, the day and night."

We have but language for the starry Heaven,
And words for continents and emperors.
I have but images within my heart
And words with which to make those images
Form in the minds of others, and, alas,
You are too wonderful and beautiful,
I cannot tell the marvel of your land,
But can be happy with my memories.

I think at first of cities bright with flowers,
Flowers for everybody, everywhere;
Then of a grass unlike the English turf,
"Buffalo grass," you called it, tough and springy;
Then of the birds, the exquisite blue wrens,
The kookaburras laughing in the fig-tree,
The whip birds slashing in the rainy glen,
The blue and scarlet parrots rushing past,
And black swans on the lake at Woolongoon.
Yet of the birds the black-backed magpie seems
The very soul of the Australian scene.
Often in early morning I would hear him

In strange, sweet song, now like to jingling glasses,
Now piping, now like flutes, but always telling
Of morning coming over the world's rim.
Then I remember how upon the hill,
Among the gumtrees, on the holiday,
The car sped past a sunny group of children,
And on the instant as we hurried past,
I heard a little girl cry, "There's John Masefield,"
And knew upon the instant what a power
A language has to give a fellowship
Over the distances of earth and sea.

Next, I remember how the forest stood;
Mile after mile of giant gums, blue-gray,
Glen after glen, blue-gray; peak after peak;
With blackened rampikes from old forest fires,
And bones of dead gums, white as skeletons,
And silence everywhere, not to be broken,
Save by the water in the gully talking.

Then, the great spaces like the Berkshire downs;
Mile after mile, with clumps upon the skyline
Of gumtrees which at distance looked like beech;
The wind-swept, rolling plain, dotted with sheep;
The station buildings here and there: few men,
Perhaps two children upon pony back,
Turning a mob of cattle, or the slow,
Part staggering figures of two sundowners,

Bent underneath the long rolls of their blueys,
Silently moving to a camping-place.

Next, as it were a river of bright flowers
In Earth's most lovely garden, and great rain
Ceasing above a multitude, and sun
Struggling through cloud, and lighting up the scene
Of splendid horses going to the post.
Then in the quagmire of the course, the thunder
Of the great race's passing, with surmise
From all those thousands, of which rider led;
Nothing but distant, flitting, coloured caps,
Shewed in a bunch along the rail; then, lo,
They swerved into the Straight, the great horse leading.
He bore topweight; the going was a bog;
He strode at ease, ahead, his ears still cocked.
Had he been called-upon he could have won
By half-a-mile, it seemed: his image stays
Forever in my mind as one of Power
That achieves easily while Weakness strives.

Next, I remember all the sun-swept, wind-swept
Hills of the pasture up above the brook;
No fence in sight; the cattle in small groups
Moving and grazing in the same direction,
And all the landscape stretching on and on,
To unknown mountains, forty miles away,
Where sheep and dogs and cattle, all gone wild,
Ran in the range, men said, and dingoes throve.

There was an ancient tree outside the station,
Which marked (they said) an English convict's grave.
He swallowed stolen jewels and so died.
Often I hope that that free space and light
Have freed him to the lovely universe,
So that he rides upon the wind there, singing
For joy that the old iron of his sins
Is snapped in pieces from his fettered soul.

Always above these memories is the sense
Of charming people, ever kind and thoughtful;
Most generous in thought, in word, in deed,
And faithful in their kindness to the end.
The mind is glad with many memories
Of kind things done and uttered by the race,
Earth's newest race of men, whose bodies' beauty
Surpasses all the peoples of the world;
Whose grace and care and generosity
Though never thanked, can never be forgotten.
A marvellous kind people, beautiful.

I shut my eyes and hear the magpies utter
Their magical, sweet cry like jingling glass,
And see the barren with the whited bones
Of gumtrees stretching to the flood-water,
Where black swans straddle in a line, like men
Pretending to be swans. Beyond the flood
There are the shearing sheds, where men of Anzac,

The shearers about whom the ballads tell,
Wonderful men whose fame this country treasures,
Strip off the fleeces from the sheep as though
Each fleece were but a woolly coat unbuttoned.

And many many other memories come,
Of cities fairer than our country holds;
Of waters gushing among blue-gray gums;
Or mighty pastures, each with lonely horsemen
Loping the morning, singing as they go;
Of beaches where the sun-tanned dare the sharks;
Or bush, the same for miles, all feathery-dim,
Each fathom of it green-gray, feathery-dim,
(Distinct, yet indistinct, almost like seaweed),
Where thirst has killed her hundreds, and will kill.

But among all these memories I hear
From gumtrees dead or blossoming, the magpies,
With that strange song so moving and so sweet,
The very voice of that far distant land,
So sweet that all who hear it must be moved
To hear it once again before they die.

The Will

By Will, Man dared in den and heath
The dagger-claws and sabre-teeth
And brought their savageries beneath.

By Will, he beat the flint to fire
And burned the jungle in his ire
And lit the dark to his desire.

By Will, his spirit tamed the force
Of the wild bull and the wild horse
And the wild river in her course.

By Will, he quarried and made bright
Stone spires lifting into light
With visions of the infinite.

By Will, he made him eyes to see
The Death that Kills in secrecy
From fly and louse and gnat and flea.

By Will, he made him slaves with hands
That without word do his commands
In air, in oceans and in lands.

Earth, water, air and brute and fool,
And crazy rebel against rule
By Will, he made each one his tool.

And shall he not, by Will, attack,
The country's shame, the peoples' lack,
The rags upon the nation's back?

The blots upon the nation's mind
The ignorance that makes us blind
The hate, that shuts us from our Kind?

Surely, by Will, he will blow clear
His trumpets that all ears shall hear,
And helping angels shall sweep near,

And the banners of the soul advance,
Up, out of hate and ignorance,
Into a new inheritance.

Westminster Hall

What glory and reversal has been shown
Between this paving and the roof o'erhead,
What battle between subject and the throne,
What turbulence and passion of men dead.

Ten generations have not yet gone by
Since rebels faced their King within this Hall,
With men at arms and forgery and lie
Outrageously pursuing to his fall.

Here, lit by this same window, sat the Court.
Pacing this very pavement, side to side,
The sentries took tobacco and made sport,
Keeping the rebels peace for regicide.

Somewhere within this Hall, where words and show
Masked the accursed purpose blackly laid,
Two heroisms happened good to know,
Two women spoke when England was afraid.

First, Lady Fairfax; then, a nobler heart,
Anna De Lille, who cried, that, "In this case,
The Nation, of King's subjects, had no part,
But only traitors banded and most base."

And here the traitor guards, in open court,
Yet without trial, heating irons red,

Branded her, scalp and shoulder, in such sort
They scarred "a handfull broad," a witness said.

Thereon, the fifty-nine, with sword and mace,
Sat in their Monarch's presence and preferred
Their charge ungrounded to its end sans grace,
The truth unanswered and the right unheard.

Then, after doom, the soldiers, gathered close,
Flouted and spat upon their King, and beat
The loyal few (for there were some of those),
And bore him forth in tumult to the street.

*   *   *

Nearly three hundred years have sifted by
Their pounds of rubbish for the penny just,
Since this same sun within his winter sky
Surveyed the sins of that forgotten dust.

Unnumbered sparks of the eternal soul
Have come within these doors in guise of men,
But among all those payers of Death's toll,
No English King has trodden here since then,

Until this Springtime, when the Three Estates
From Britain's soil and Britains over-sea,
Annulling here that evil of old hates,
Welcomed their King and Queen in Jubilee.

29

Here, where the rebels doomed their King, the Peers
Gave grateful thanks to God for King and Queen.
The Commons shook the ancient roof with cheers.
O happy King and people; happy scene.

Ballet Russe

I

The gnome from moonland plays the Chopin air,
The ballerina glides out of the wings,
Like all the Aprils of forgotten Springs.
Smiling she comes, all smile,
All grace; forget the cruel world awhile:
Forget vexation now and sorrow due.
A blue cap sits coquettish in her hair.

She is all youth, all beauty, all delight,
All that a boyhood loves and manhood needs.
What if an Empire perishes, who heeds?
Smiling she comes, her smile
Is all that may inspire, or beguile.
All that our haggard folly thinks untrue.
Upon the trouble of the moonlit strain
She moves like living mercy bringing light.

Soon, when the gnomish fingers cease to stray,
She will be gone, still smiling, to the wings,
To live among our unforgotten things,
Centaur and unicorn,
The queens in Avalon and Roland's horn,
The mystery, the magic and the dew
Of a to-morrow and a yesterday.

II

With delicate control in maddest speed
This rocket shoots and falls, and falling, twists;
Where Nature has denied, his soul insists:
Grace, strength and skill are fused.
Thus has the starry skill his matter used,
The harsh, rebellious, formless, lineless stuff
That would not soon obey, nor blend, nor heed.

This leapt above the horns or bulls in Crete;
This hunted Hector round the walls of Troy;
This brought the god into his shrine in joy;
Thus, long ago, began
Whatever beauty has begun in man,
The image being beaten from the rough,
In hungry instants by the incomplete.

Joseph Hodges, or The Corn

He wore the smock-frock of the country's past,
That ancient with frank eye and upright head;
His gray hair, beautiful unto the last,
Nearly upon his withered shoulders spread.
He had a stubbly beard, his furrowed cheeks
Were bloodless Age's, threaded with red streaks.

He, who had gathered eighty harvests in
As boy or reaper, now himself was white
For Death to sickle and to bring to bin.
Gone was his body's old companion, Might.
He, who had all day sung, swinging his hook,
Now waited to be carted, a cut stook.

His hands, that long had hardened on the hale,
Holding the plough behind two horses' backs,
And in the sheds of old had swung the flail
On many a harvest, now lay white and lax.
Himself sat upright ever, gazing forth
Over the grass and hopyards to the north.

What harvest did his inner eyes behold
From his spent Summer, now that Winter came?
The women who had cherished him of old?
The friends whom ninety Autumns had made tame?
The ploughteams pondering out, on shaggy hoofs,
At dawn, from farms with pigeons on their roofs?

These; and, perhaps, some feeling of the link
Of Destiny, that bound him to the Corn,
Beauty and bounty of man's meat and drink,
That greens, and browns, and then is waggon-borne,
And then is food, and strength, and then is Joy,
Seed-corn of crops that nothing can destroy.

For, as a man declines toward the tomb,
The symbols of his life, that ruled his way
Before his spirit quickened in the womb,
Gather to cheer him through his hut's decay,
So haply here, as darkness gathered dim,
Immortal cornland shone, and nourished him.

Till, as he gazed into the past, the sound,
The scene and colour of his life's delight,
The crop in April, green upon the ground,
The crop in rank, in bristle, sickle-white,
The crop in barn, in bread, all merged and made
A Word that led him deathwards unafraid.

*   *   *   *   *

It is raw clay tangled with roots of flowers.
This earth that grows the grass and little flowers.
You cut it with the share or with the spade;
It is like meat, it shines; the stones stick in it.
The seed is flung on it and tumbled over,
While the rooks' beaks, like iron, probe for it,
And gulls' bills too; and bitter winter binds.

Then, in the dark meat of the world, the seed
Heats in its nook, and sings, and thrusts out roots
To suck and clutch, to break in three and suck.
Then, feeling where the sun shines, it arises
And bursts out of the clod into the Spring,
The sun, the sky, the blowing cloud and wind,
Rain falling mixed with snowflakes; blackthorn blowing.

First, fear of birds' beaks and of hunters' hooves,
Then the green blade will cover up the hare
As she lies, furrow to the kestrel's eye.

Then, as the cuckoo comes and May rain follows
With hawthorn, crimson speckled, drowsy smelling,
It stands and buds and ears, till it is army
Massed within hedges, dense as a King's crowd.
The vixen with her cubs lie in the runway
Watching the shrew-mice race into the dark,
Or beetles rambling, or the harvest-mice
Weaving their ball of joy above bright stems.

Two sparks among the rust of a red fur,
One with the clay, the vixen: rabbits come
Nibble the nicked tongues of the milky weed,
And scratch, or cock an ear, or rise to listen
With drooped forepaws, and round eyes very bright.
High overhead the sparrow-hawk is watching.

His murder drops, the footpad weasel leaps,
The white trap of the vixen snatches suddenly.
There is a squealing, bleating into silence.
A blackbird chackers: all begins again,
Under high summer blazing in the sun
In a great drone of flies, now up, now down.
Sometimes a little boy, escaped from school,
Creeps up the ditch and thence into the forest
Of countless yellowing stems; he sits there, hidden
Marvelling at the dusk close to the ground
Smiling to hear his fellows call his name
Not knowing where he is; but not replying
Till they, weary of calling, having tasted
The honey in the honeysuckle trumpets
Among the hedge close-by, go shouting on,
While he sits still, within the amber gloom
Seeing far off the head and crimson eye
Of a cock pheasant, lifted, watching him,
And near at hand the delicate strong strings
(Decked with striped flowers) that twist about the stalks;
Rough poppy stems with scarlet banners drooped;
Blue cornflower and yellow ragwort flowers
And thistle tufting into down for finches.

At dusk, with silent glide of curving wings,
The covey settle and run swift, swift, swift,
Into their quiet, where the mottled shells
Lie broken, whence they came. Now the moon rises,

The owls come out; the moths with their long tongues
Quiver above the honey-suckle trumpets.
The humble bees beside their honey-pouches
Dream of the clover-field in the hot light,
Ten acres of pink clusters of sweet suck.
A white mist dims on the cool grass and thickens
Above the pond, along the water-reach.
Night deepens and is still, save for some cow
Moving in pasture, or the squeak of bats,
Or bells from the two churches within hearing,
Or sheep in fold above, cropping the chicory.

But when the dew is gone, on the hot morrow
Farmer and men and teams come with the reapers;
And all day long the horses drag the reapers
Swathe within swathe along the lessening square.
The army falls in rank, the flowers wither,
And men and women stook the banded bundles,
And then with sticks and guns murder the rabbits
That have crept inwards to the last patch cut.
The dusk falls on a field of tented stooks
Where wild things tremble at the covert gone,
And partridges call each to each till darkness.

Now, the brown horses drag the waggons in
For loading of the stooks, till all is carted.
All the rough, bristling, four square plaited ears
All fat and firm with food, are flung aloft;

Then the last bundle of the last stook taken
Falls to the woman, for her plait, then all,
Men, women, children, mount on the last waggon,
Waving their wisps of gleaning, and all sing
In the hot afternoon, for harvest home.
The wheels crush the close stubble, the song lifts,
In joy of earth that makes man's marrow fat
And cords his muscles; joy of the sun that pours
Energy forth on life, joy of the corn,
By which their twinned strength enters into man.
So with their song they come into the barn;
There the brown mice flit to the golden shelter
And pigeons pick the spilled grain, the red cock
Clucks for his wives; they peck about the floor.
But the skilled woman plaits from the last stook
Twin crowns of straw, for Gospel and Epistle,
To hang in Church upon Thanksgiving day.

Soon, when the apples redden or glow gold,
And hawthorn berries brighten in the hedge,
And partridges are killed and swallows gather,
The threshers will be there, and all day long
The drone will lift and die about the farm
Among the wash and trample of flung straw,
The dust of straw, the heaving forks of men,
Chaff underfoot and bodies of dead mice,
While the sacked grain is readied for the mill.

*   *   *

All-living Sun, all-giving Earth, the two
Father and Mother of the stock of men,
Kindler and giver of the miracle
By which we stand, the Corn, we give Thee thanks.

By Corn we eat the radiance of high heaven
And inmost blood and marrow of the earth;
All that the easter chills and wester fosters;
All that the will of life within the seed
Can suck of plumpness from the clay; of greenness
Out of the air, the rain, or resolved atom;
Of ripeness from the turning of the wheel.

This that was plant of pride is now man's strength,
Steering a ploughshare steady between horses;
Leading the bull to drink; sickling laid corn;
Mowing the knee-deep meadow of moon-daisies,
In the June blaze among the biting flies,
When cuckoos try for their forgotten tune;
Holding the stallion in his hour of ramp;
Sinking the piers of bridges, laying causeways
Athwart the run of floods, damming back tides,
Winning a cornland from the sea itself;
Daring the sea on fallen logs, fire-hollowed,
Then, daring further, felling pine and oak
Bending the stubborn timber, sawing plank,
Pitching the seams and launching forth with oars,
Or canvas hoisted, to the unknown fate
Beyond the skyline, out of sight of land.

And from this mettle of man, the sweetness comes:
The women with the majesty of queens,
With knowledge, mercy, wisdom; their calm eyes
Perceiving truth, their courage sheltering truth,
Their selflessness like light about men's lives,
Their tenderness like light to little children,
Who sport about them, singing, merry as May.

All strength and gladness, shadows of Earth and Sun,
Are shadows of the might and glory of God,
To Whom all men who grow out of the Earth
Lift in their exultation, as the Corn lifts.

Out of this Corn, that is such joy, men build
Their churches, where they act day after day
With singing, music, dancing, lights and colour,
The death and resurrection of glad man,
Till the eared corn of man becomes a flame
No longer Earth, but burning from the Sun,
No longer multitudinous but one,
No longer bread of sacrifice but Joy.

The Wild Geese

All the Many is One,
In each Father is Son,
On one string the beads run.

In each Sister is Brother,
In each Daughter is Mother,
All Each is Other.

Since I am You, You, Me,
Why scarlet Earth and Sea
With noun of Be?

      *   *   *

Salt Severn shines in strip,
The Wild Geese poise at lip,
One web at hip.

Bright eyes open on brain,
There are things in the rain,
It's danger again.

A clanking, a roar, a rise,
Multitude, with hounds' cries,
Flag, flog, in skies.

Away, away, in huddles,
Shadows shoot in the puddles,
The grey cloud cruddles.

Fly, pennon, and clank, pen,
Your bread is the salt fen,
Your laughter, at Men.

On bread of trash of the seas,
In laughter of soul go these,
But they are only Wild Geese.

*   *   *

I saw, in Delville Wood,
A cat lap a man's blood,
A cat eat a man's brain.
Men want to see't again.

*   *   *

All Winter through they ravenge
The salprey's glitter, for scavenge,
Any findings are havings.

All i'the mud, i'the dark,
With one wit warm, they hark
The tide run, the fox bark.

Candlemas-fox stops tune,
Wild geese go by the moon,
Sickle-edge is too soon.

Snowdrop-moon, grown, reminds
Of highways over the winds
To snows one finds.

42

They listen, they quest with bill,
As moon grows, the bloods thrill,
Then, away with a will.

Up, up, round, and away,
A hurricane of grey,
Droppt breast-feathers as spray.

Past sea-blink and sea-coast,
This arrow hurls, this host,
Of will-flung ghost.

Till, there, ice, ice, forlorn,
Where no grass grows, nor corn,
Nor men dead nor man born.

Down, where the shark-mouth steals,
By black ice-holes, for seals,
The flight hurls, the flock wheels.

They light by green ice-pools.
None, of them all, such fools,
As to be ruled; none rules.

A long long crying and gabble,
Running forward in rabble,
Broad bills nibble and scrabble.

The Northern Lights behold
Their nesting in the cold,
Their goslings gold.

* * *

Dusk falls when the Sun turns,
Frost strangles with white ferns,
A redness burns.

The Sun is dead in the South,
A hunger calls and a drouth
For sea-mud salt i'the mouth.

Then away, hurling, afar,
No Sun, no Moon, no Star,
Yet marshes are.

They have no masses, no classes,
No wars, no poison-gasses,
They are geese, they are asses.

O, it must be absurd
To be a goose of a bird
And salute no general spurred.

Civilisation rots
When men aren't killed with shots.
Souls grow rustic and mothic
Unless kept cut-throat and gothic;

44

It is the fact, all know it,
Except these geese and that poet.

If we could put goose-brain
In airship or aeroplane,
We could drop bombs like rain.

Make such holes in the mud,
Fill them full with such blood,
Give God thanks for Security,
Practice Racial Purity,
And be (if God should please),
Almost as wise as geese.

Hope

O Hope that glimmers in the breast
Come within Life, be manifest.
  Make better best.

Change us, that we no longer lie
Living in ignorance, nor die
  In poverty.

Take, first, the thought (of Hell's contrival)
Of Man, Man's Enemy and Rival,
  Back to the devil.

And bring again from Heaven the thought
Of Man, Man's Brother, whom Christ bought
  In His fight fought.

The Queen

I waited, in my misery, when the Queen,
The Queen herself, unclasped the heavy gold,
Flung back the cloak and gave it me to hold:
"You serve us here to-night," she said. I told
Through what long deaths of sorrow I had been.

Then she: "Though misery come or misery go,
The Queen is, ever: mortals serve her still
Through flood like sea or fire like a hill,
And when the body perish, by the will;
You, though you sorrow, serve us even so."

And ah, she smiled: I took the golden cloak,
So heavy with its splendour, thinking this:—
"Our service for immortal beauty is . . .
O what are pain, death, sorrow, miseries?
I'll serve till the heart break and the voice choke."

Beauty

O Queen of Beauty, you who once were fire
In hearts, in every city, till they wrought
The image of you out of passionate thought,
Their only peace the ecstasy you brought,
Their only life the dying from desire,

If men have changed, immortal you are still
The snowdrop in the February grass,
The stormcock crying that the snow will pass,
The Hope, to breaking souls that say "Alas,"
Crying, "Come, courage, luck will change, it will."

You are still that, O Beauty, you are ours
As Hope, as some wild knocker at the door,
Entering, dropping snow upon the floor,
With word of Kingdoms never known before;
And strong hearts kindle, and the watch-dog cowers.

February Night

I went into the land where Beauty dwells.
The winter darkness shut it as a prison.
The thin moon, due at midnight, had not risen.
The clouds moved slowly over: nothing else
Stirred, nor did owl cry, nor did glow-worm glisten.
The night in all her vastness stood to listen.
Then, in the valley church, men rang the bells.

Out of the tower into the winter air
They shook their triumph: and a hill beyond
Made laggard ghosts of echoes to respond.
As turbulent water beats the boulder bare
And hurries and leaps, so turbulent drin and drone
Clanged and were spilled in cataracts of tone
Out of the tower above the ringers there.

Then the bells ceased; the men, as I suppose
Muffling their throats in woollens, trudged to bed.
The Heaven displayed her star-work overhead
Star beyond star, the brighter as it froze.
A fox barked thrice, none answered, the world slept,
Save at some oven where a cricket kept
Trilling the drowsy cat into a doze.

February Morning

The starry wheel of night passed slowly over;
Then, in the East, the grayness became red.
The hills with all their forest lifted head.
Like skeletons of leaves in every cover
The tapering twigs arose on each elm-arm.
Out of the cattle yard of Sorrel's Farm
A lad came driving, singing like a lover.

He stood to drive, he urged the horse, he swayed
About the bend, the rough haired cob and he,
The yellow milk-float's grincing axle tree
Just missed the gate-post in the turn he made.
The cob snorted and shook his head and went
Up to the collar: and the driver leant
Like youth the warrior on a cattle-raid.

He was fair-haired, bare-headed, cheery-eyed
Going, full-pace, into the morning, singing,
While overhead the myriad birds were winging;
A rosy sun hove over the hill-side.
The singing of the driver was of love:—
"O she is fairer than the sun above"
He carolled clear "And she shall be my bride."

Nets

COLONIES built a fort for safety's sake,
With red-brick barracks, near the marshy lake.

When it was finished GOVERNMENT proclaimed,
"Lakes within mile of barracks must be drained."

BARRACKS objected on financial grounds,
"Draining the lake will cost five thousand pounds."

GOVERNMENT answered: *"In re Drainage . . . stet.
Fix doors and windows with mosquito net."*

*"Order the needed net on Indent Three . . .
MEDICAL TROPICAL . . . DEPARTMENT D."*

BARRACKS took Indent Three and read the rules
Printed atop by imbeciles for fools.

BARRACKS took measures: after many days
Completed indents went upon their ways.

The sailors bore them safely over sea,
The postman brought them to DEPARTMENT D.

DEPARTMENT D replied: *"Re nets required . . .
Reply per memo:—meshes stringed or wired?"*

BARRACKS replied: *"Your favour, seventh, rec't*
In view of white ant, wire meshes best."

DEPARTMENT D retorted in reply:
"For wire mesh indent DEPARTMENT I."

BARRACKS replied: *"To save time, kindly send*
Indents you hold DEPARTMENT I, your end."

DEPARTMENT D replied: *"See Orders A.*
Indent the proper Dep't in proper way."

BARRACKS replied: *"To save re-measurement,*
Kindly return the No. 3 Indents sent."

DEPARTMENT D replied: *"The Indents are*
Filed, as per Regs., see Six, Jacobus R."

BARRACKS again made indents: in the task
Reams of spoiled papers filled the paper-bask'.

The sailors bore the indents, clean and dry;
The postman gave them to DEPARTMENT I.

DEPARTMENT I immediate answer made:
"Report why Requisition thus delayed

"Surprised and shocked that Orders urgent plain
Ignored and flouted. What excuse? Explain."

52

DEPARTMENT I made ring a hundred bells,
A hundred subs passed on a thousand hells,

A thousand willing workers wrought as one,
Windows and doors, the netted frames were done.

The sailors bore them safely in their carracks,
The lorry men delivered them to BARRACKS.

BARRACKS announced: *"Re Nets. Acknowledge same.
Parade with small arms for Mosquito Frame."*

Battalions mustered: sergeants' voices hoarse
Shouted *"Form Fours. Squad, as you were. Form Fours."*

The netted frames were issued: every file
Formed Fours, saluted, Right-wheeled to the pile,

Took each a frame, Formed Fours, saluted, Formed
Fours and Right Dressed, as when a city's stormed.

Soon from the ranks the question passed along:
"How do we fasten frames where they belong?"

Captains considered, majors looked perplexed,
Colonels, not knowing, could, by rank, be vexed.

The LINE, not knowing, asked the HORSE; the sons
Of Pegasus, the HORSE said: *"Ask the Guns."*

The GUNS replied: *"We know not. It appears*
An Ironmonger's job: Ask ENGINEERS."

The ENGINEERS replied: *"By Barrack Square,*
We do not do mechanics: Ask the AIR."

The AIR replied: *"The methods most in use*
Are: Nails (the cheapest); Hooks and Eyes; or Screws."

"Right," said COMMAND: *"Parade. The Order is:*
Pile all Mosquito Frames. Form Fours. Dismiss.

"And for the Frames, we'll do as AIR advise,
Indent the proper Dep't for Hooks and Eyes."

The Frames were piled: the BARRACKS searched the
      Books
Of Rules prescribing Forms for ordering Hooks.

One said: *"For Hooks, 3, William IV, applies:*
Or seems to do, but not for Hooks and Eyes."

Another said: *"But by Department Rules*
Hooks count as Doctor's Comforts, Eyes as Tools."

Another said: *"Appeal Court makes it good*
That Eyes are Ordnance Stores and Hooks are Food."

Another said: *"War Regulations say*
Both are Munitions, needing Buff Form A."

Another said: *"Defence Acts: Section P . . .*
Says they're both Rations, needing Blue Form G."

Another said: *"Why go to all the fuss?*
Malarial Fever never troubles us.

"Malarial Fever never has been known
Within the Circuit: leave the thing alone."

"Why nets?" another cried, *"As I'm a sinner . . .*
Why rob the poor mosquito of his dinner?

"That cannot stop a poison in the air
Invisible, and blowing everywhere."

Another said: *"Ours not to reason why:*
Let's get our own back on DEPARTMENT I."

The Message went: *"Mosquito Nets to hand.*
No Hooks nor Eyes. We cannot understand.

"Is this incompetence, or is it worse,
Wilful betrayal of the public purse?

"COMMAND and COLONIES await with pain
Eyes, Hooks, Apologies: Express. Explain."

55

DEPARTMENT I replied: *"Rule Ninety-six*
Says MEDICAL gives Nets, but BARRACKS fix.

"Fix as you please, your cost, nor bother thus
With senile prate. Hooks no concern of us."

BARRACKS appealed to COLONIES: *"Reply*
Following cable from DEPARTMENT I.

"Urge you request Department to provide
Fixings omitted with the Nets supplied.

"Nettings as furnished useless until placed,
And Fever season near: no time to waste."

COLONIES cabled, the DEPARTMENT wrote
To STATE DEPARTMENT, LAW: *"Attention. Note.*

"MEDICAL TROPICAL are asked for Eyes
And Hooks with Nettings. We refuse. Advise."

LAW (STATE DEPARTMENTS), said: *"Act Seven,*
    Four,
Edward the Second, is applied no more;

"But might be pleaded: Statute, Mary, Nine,
Restraining Soldiery's a stronger line;

"And in WEST INDIA ISLANDS versus GUNS
A precedent was 'stablished, which still runs:

"Thus, that although the State may greatly grant
All things, in theory, sometimes it can't.

"And when it can't, as in the present case,
Then it devolves on officers in place

"To improvise and implement until
The State they serve is saved from threatened ill.

"This seems the likeliest line. Advise you cable
BARRACKS affix the Nets themselves if able.

"The trifling cost must be subscribed from Pay."
BARRACKS received this in the Flanders way.

They cabled LAW DEPARTMENT, ARMY BRANCH:
"MEDICAL TROPICAL makes boldest blanch.

They urge us pay, or plainly so intend,
For Hooks they should have sent and didn't send.

"Urge that such quibbling be at once opposed."
LAW (ARMY BRANCH) drew battle-axe and closed.

LAW (STATE DEPARTMENTS) bowed from bitter
    thwacks
Dealt by LAW'S (ARMY BRANCH'S) battle-axe.

LAW'S (ARMY BRANCH'S) battle phalanx cried:
"Hooks are your Province, instantly provide,

"Or grant the thirty pounds that BARRACKS may."
LAW (STATE DEPARTMENTS) quavered in dismay.

MEDICAL TROPICAL, DEPARTMENT I,
Quavered as well, but rallied to reply.

They pressed LAW (STATE DEPARTMENTS) to say
    thus:
"The cost of Hooking cannot fall on us.

"Statutes and Regulations make it plain.
We shall not answer such request again."

LAW (ARMY BRANCH) applied another force;
Their BRANCH'S MEMBER rose in fitting course

And said that Honourable Members heard
Of shocking things (or shocking things averred)

Against the TROPIC BRANCH OF PUBLIC
    HEALTH.
That sickening corruptions crept by stealth

To Offices, was known: Democracy,
The Greek Sage said, must have a watchful Eye.

That, for his own part, he would never credit
A thing so grim, yet everybody said it.

He therefore hoped that Government would sift
The matter out. Enquiry should be swift.

He heard that State Officials, penny wise,
Boggled at heroes having Hooks and Eyes.

Our brave defenders under Tropic Suns
Marched Hook and Eyeless on the foemen's guns.

If it were so (he could not well believe it),
Let Justice draw her Sword and Guilt receive it.

He sat, amid applause, and as it died,
LAW'S (STATE DEPARTMENTS') Member, rose and
    sighed,

And twitched his waistcoat down and sniffed, and said,
That never yet since Parliament was made

Had charge more stealthy with more brazen brow
Been urged more basely, with less wit, than now.

The facts were plain: observing recent laws,
TROPICAL HEALTH despatched Mosquito Gauze

To BARRACKS underneath the Tropic Sun.
ALL BARRACKS fixed the Nets excepting one.

One erring BARRACKS only stood aside,
Ignoring Nets, in military pride.

This BARRACKS being taunted for neglect,
Still sought excuse for failing to erect

These necessary barriers against Death.
He had not eloquence, nor had he breath,

To character in fitting terms their error.
He mentioned it with shrinking, nay, with terror . . .

Would Members credit him? These sons of Mars,
Rich with the spoils of many frontier wars,

Refused to pay the paltry sixpence each
To fix the Nettings. Without further speech

He asked the House to let their Censure fall
Full on the erring BARRACKS, if at all.

Then, upon one side or another, rose
Members, to urge with thunder, or oppose . . .

This way and that they gave sufficient grounds
That BARRACKS pay, or not pay, thirty pounds.

GOVERNMENT lastly rose and said, in fact,
That something somewhere contravened the Act;

That faults were better probed, not by Division,
But grave enquiry by a staid Commission.

That such Commission should be promptly named
To settle who should pay and which be blamed.

Straightway the Members of Commission sat
And heard how that was this and this was that;

And heard the Leaders of DEPARTMENT I
Refuse to pay, since they would rather die.

While BARRACKS cabled, first, that Metal Hooks
Were Comforts for the Sick in all the Books:

That Metal Eyes, by all the Regulations,
Were stores for Casualty Clearing Stations:

And that as Stores or Comforts they would all
Die, ere they paid, so let the Heavens fall.

Meanwhile the Netted Frames in quiet heaps
Sheltered the barrack kittens' mid-day sleeps.

And Time went by, who grieves not nor exults
But passes and in passing brings results.

Mosquitos came and bit; the fever crept
Into the veins of soldiers as they slept,

And fever rose till every other bed
Held one who babbled from a throbbing head.

And some men died, and half a full platoon,
As weak as pith and pallid as the moon,

Were invalided-out, and shipped away
To England, never more to hear the bray

Of bugle, sergeant, knight or colonel.
The fever burned the Barracks to a shell:

All were as ghosts, who lived, and in their veins
Still, to this day, the living death remains.

The general, shuddering with fever-quake,
Wrote out the Order: *"We must drain the Lake."*

When it was drained, the COLONIES reported
To GOVERNMENT: *"Let BARRACKS be transported*

"Across the Island to another site."
GOVERNMENT wrote: *"Suggestion good. Invite*

"Tenders forthwith. Shift BARRACKS across Isle."

62

The Government Commission sat meanwhile
Hearing the Experts on Mosquito Net
And Hooks and Eyes.
            I'm told they're sitting yet.

The Long Drive

(Edinburgh to Boar's Hill)

In a garage not far from the Rock of the Castle
I saw the car ready and filled all her tanks.
As the clocks chimed for eight I turned into the bustle,
And the air flitted swift past the little car's flanks.

We were soon past the lights of the city's mean alleys
And standing away as the darkness closed in,
The hills glowed and faded, the lamps starred the valleys,
We heard the last lark, and the first owl begin.

With glaring on glaring of motor-cars homing,
The road lighted up till the glarer was past;
The still-breathing midnight stole into the gloaming,
The motors grew fewer and ended at last.

At times in the townships from windows bright lighted,
Came music, or singing, but these soon were few;
Now a bicyclist passed, now a walker benighted,
Now a policeman on beat going caped from the dew.

Then lamplight grew scarcer, each village we entered
Was a blind row of homes at each side of the street,
With a croucht, green-eyed cat going stealthy self-centred.
On the shrieking of mice under rose-briar feet.

Then we entered a darkness where no-one was stirring,
The moths moved and drooped in the beam of our light,
Now a leaf struck the hood, or a beetle went whirring,
Or a dazed rabbit leaped and was lost in the night.

Then the way became one with the night, lost and lonely;
Through moorland and woodland and downland we
    hurled;
We were swift-running light on a reach of road only,
And to swerve right or left, that alone was the world.

Then lamplight shewed steady, our hurry was slackened,
We drove the still street of a fast-asleep town,
Not a dog barked to greet us, the world ahead blackened,
And again we beat on through the wind on the down.

Unknown and unseen were the moorlands beside us,
The railway to England lay close to the road,
White signal posts stood, having round lamps that eyed us,
The telegraph wires were arrows that glowed.

Then with roaring and rush, and a spilling glare shaking,
On the railway beside us the Scotsman went by;
The moon stepped in stillness, her white fleece forsaking,
A planet burned bright in the south-western sky.

They burned, moon and planet, in heaven before us,
An unchanging change sped away as I scanned.

My engine beat time and the gear whined in chorus,
The wheel's pressure shifted to right or left hand.

Then lo, as we hurried, an inn by the wayside,
Red petrol-pumps ranged and a dusty parked car,
Two travellers halting for beds till the day-tide,
And a man bearing bags to the lighted inn-bar.

And halting, myself, till the porter could tend me,
I filled up my tanks, but resolved not to stay;
Since the wind and the planet and moon would be-
     friend me
I dreaded no moor-mist nor missing the way.

So to Beattock (for Moffat) I held, past the gleaming
Bright stars in the bog-pools, scared peewits that rose,
Bright waters in spate from the hill torrents streaming,
And the startled strange crying of sheep on the knowes.

Past Beattock's dark moorland of curlew and plover,
Past Moffat, and on, through the wind striking cold,
Past the granite-strown moors where Carlyle was a lover,
Where his blithe wife and he rode together of old.

There he pondered the doings of men, and gave sentence,
And felt the winged spirit dragged back by the chain,
Rejoiced in his might and stood sick in repentance,
Bareheaded alone on the moors in the rain.

Beyond Ecclefechan, the lowlands drew nearer,
The hills shrank to levels, a water gleamed wan,
The wheel moved and backed to the will of the steerer,
The ever-lapped roadway for ever led on.

Till lo, there, before us, were black bulks of grimness,
The bridge and the castle and town of Carlisle.
We drove through her silence, then paused in the dimness
To eat, and drink coffee, and rest us awhile.

And then, since I came to those roads as a stranger,
I bent to the sidelights to study the map,
And thought of the warnings of friends of the danger
Of loose shifting surface at bends upon Shap.

I thought of the Romans who marched up to battle
Along the same road, and of Scots who had come
Twixt midnight and dawn for the reiving of cattle,
Or for Stuart and crown with the bagpipe and drum.

They had come, they had gone, with their fervour and
    order,
Their hope and their song and the sergeant's swift curse,
To the end God ordained them; that place was the
    Border,
Men crossed it like marriage, for better or worse.

Then away once again by the ways given over
To darkness and silence and things of the night,

Where the glaring green eyes showed the fox was a rover,
And the hedgehogs' long legs ran like stilts from the light.

And the eyes of the hedgehogs were red to our seeming,
And the cats' eyes gleamed green, near the lightless still
    homes.
We drove by a wood where the rabbits were teeming,
The hedgehogs among them went hunchbacked like
    gnomes.

Then we drew to the lakes and the beauty of waters,
And mountains and forest and moonlit still bays;
Night brooded above with the planets her daughters,
Their light on the waters made magical ways.

I thought that those waters had mirrored the faces
Of a brother and sister, most dear to us still,
He, stern as the crags and as deep as their bases,
She, calm with a love that no evil can kill.

They lived with those mountains and lakes till the brother
Was one with their spirit and spoke with their voice,
And April herself laid her hand on the other
And gave her her power to bless and rejoice.

The water that mirrored their faces, the grasses
They trod on, have gone, as their bodies have gone,
But power vouchsafed to a soul never passes,
And beauty once given forever lives on.

Beside, as we sped, was a cataract lashing,
Then darkness and silence of mountains and trees,
Then lakes black with shadow, with mirrored stars
    flashing,
And fir-forest voiced like the breaking of seas.

Then I thought that beside me a swift foot had trodden,
And a clear voice had echoed from each of those rocks,
John Peel in the dew in his homespun gray hodden
Had come with his hounds there and wakened the fox.

For Troutbeck was near us, where once, in the morning,
The horn of John Peel had aroused men to mirth;
We thought of that hunter we passed Troutbeck horning,
Though he and his meyny were long gone to earth.

Then on, growing weary as night became older,
The wheel swayed and altered: we speeded or slowed
The road swerved and reswerved to this or that shoulder,
Our goal was the light on the bend in the road.

The darkness was chill as the sky paled for morning,
Then colour came shyly, the trees became green,
A blackbird flew out from the hedge with a warning,
I switched off the lights for the road could be seen.

Lamps burned in the bedrooms, the world was awaking,
Near Lancaster city we passed the first man.

Ere we left him behind us the morning was breaking,
And soon all about us the day's work began.

Then we came into Preston and halted an hour,
And bathed and had breakfast and shifted a rim,
Then cleaned up her spark-plugs and filled her with
    power,
And headed her south through the dark towns and grim.

Till to right there were towers, soot-blackened, smoke-
    spouting,
Below them the masting of steamers at piers,
Steam plucking the tackles of derricks, men shouting,
And fat, spinning slings lapsing landward with cheers.

We passed them; beyond them a bridge gave us entry
To country unsmircht by steel, cotton or coal,
A grim-looking garage beside it stood sentry,
We filled all our tanks and went on for our goal.

The hot summer morning grew brighter before us,
Green farms lay beside us, clear blue was the sky,
With swift steady beating the engine kept chorus,
And village by village the landmarks dropped by.

All crowded the road was, and narrow, and winding,
Ten bends to a furlong and most of them blind,
The sun dead ahead in his southing was blinding,
But landmark by landmark the towns dropped behind.

Till presently, blue in the distance, the presence,
"The old Shropshire mountain," the Wrekin, raised head,
The god with his wolf, waiting grim in his pleasance
With churchyards all round him where Masefields lie
     dead.

We halted near Newport: the drive had gone slowly
From press on the road, and the way little known,
Now here nothing passed, but a grocer's van solely
That ran by for Shifnal and left us alone.

Most sweet was the hot summer drowse as we rested,
But Shifnal to Oxford meant many miles still.
I went through her spark-plugs and cleaned them and
     tested,
And climbed back aboard and went on with a will.

Two miles beyond Shifnal, the road gangs were tarring,
The width of the roadway was wet with hot tar,
A driver sped by us and sent it all starring
In black flicks and splashes all over the car.

Mist clung here and there as the summer day ended,
We drew near to Severn, but now on the road
With barking of sheep dogs the milking-cows wended
From meadow to byre and often we slowed.

By the red sandstone rocks under Bridgnorth the olden,
By Bowman, we went, through the fast dying day,

As we neared Kidderminster the sunset was golden,
When the car ceased to run there, the twilight was gray.

After halting and working, the engine re-started;
We drove across Bromsgrove, through Redditch and on.
The day (and the joy of the drive) had departed,
And all save the effort to end it was gone.

At Alcester, we passed gipsy caravans going
To camp by some copse on their way to a fair,
A glimpse of lit windows and foreign eyes showing,
And ponies with ears back and yellow teeth bare.

At Stratford we halted to dine at the Arden,
The full night had deepened with stars in the sky.
The oars of the boatmen who rowed past the garden
Made ruffles of glitter go loitering by.

Then on, for the last lap, though aching and dizzy,
The last fifty miles, through the moonless dark hours;
A crowd seemed about me, all talking and busy,
And the road seemed a tunnel deep-burrowed through
    flowers.

And at times all the flowers arched up, tall and splendid,
Like a Gothic church roof in a vault overhead,
And I longed as I drove for the drive to be ended,
And the swift beating engine at peace in its shed.

Long Compton was passed, and the bend in the hollow,
Near Enstone, and still all the way seemed alive
With people loud-talking, all running to follow,
Till the car had more voices than bees in a hive.

Then we drooped towards Woodstock and slowed to go
        through it,
Past the old English house where the Black Prince was
        born,
I thought of the maxim—seek peace and ensue it;
I longed for my peace as a starved horse for corn.

But mixed with the longing was rapture of knowing
The four hundred miles that the wheels had whirled by,
The things swiftly seen in the scene swiftly flowing,
The fields and the homes where men struggle and die.

The glimpses of houses, of waters, of people,
The child by the roadside, the stallions' slow lurch,
The moment of chimes from the bells in a steeple,
The instant of joy from some marvellous church.

All these were as things that a man's soul remembers
Perhaps, after death, when his body lies numb,
That kindle perhaps into flame from the embers,
And lighten his soul in the next life to come.

They flashed in my spirit, they sang with their voices,
Their triumph attuned to the hurrying wheels,

73

That over all sorrow a power rejoices,
That under all laughter a sympathy feels.

Ahead, blinking lights showed the motor-cars coming,
They gleamed round the corner and glared in my face;
So suns see their planets through wide heaven homing,
So stars see the comets in infinite space.

Yet another few miles, every reach, every bending,
Each hollow and hole known and dropped in our flight,
Up the steep pitch of bridge, down the swerved slope
    descending,
Then over the rails, to the first Oxford light.

Then slow, through the long shiny way growing brighter,
The trees of St. Giles's, the lines of parked cars;
The turn for the Broad and the turn for the Mitre,
And Folly Bridge river reflecting the stars.

Then after the hill, by the wood, round the turning,
At last the white gate and the thuia's swished frond;
I sounded the klaxon for joy of returning,
And drew back the brake in the green shed beyond.

Then after the long lurching leap all was stable,
And after the glare of the lamps all was black,
And silence ticked in from the engine's long babel,
The moon above Bledlow moved white out of wrack.

Then silently out of the pine-branches o'er us
An owl floated wraith-like, like thought going by,
The mice rustled leaves in the fern-patch before us,
The owl clawed an oak-bough and fluted his cry.

The Flowing of the Sangarios

I saw a sullen little river swerve
Across the angry barren as we sped.
The land was skinned down to the naked nerve,
The war had blasted all the dwellers dead.
No building near but had its roofing spilled
Bare to the iron heaven overhead.
Gray-brown the world was without touch of spring;
The trees, the flowers and the grass were killed.

To me that landscape was a wondrous thing.

For once, in youth, King Priam, clad in bronze,
Marched by that river with the lads of Troy,
Northward, to battle with the Amazons;
And having conquered them retrod his track,
Bearing his prize; there Hecuba and he
Courted and wedded and begat their boy;
Zeus in his mercy letting neither see
The things he stewarded and meant to be:—
Helen, the busy beaches, the attack;
Skamander's water lilies red with blood;
Achilles dragging Hector in the mud;
The murder in the midnight and the sack.

Wood-Pigeons

Often the woodman scares them as he comes
Swinging his axe to split the fallen birch:
The keeper with his nim-nosed dog at search
Flushes them unaware; then the hive hums.

Then from the sheddings underneath the beech,
Where squirrels rout, the flock of pigeons goes,
Their wings like sticks in battle giving blows,
The hundred hurtling to be out of reach.

Their wings flash white above a darker fan,
In drifts the colour of the smoke they pass,
They disappear above the valley grass,
They re-appear against the woodland tan.

Now that the valley woodlands are all bare,
Their flocks drift daily thus, now up, now down,
Blue-grey against the sodden of the brown,
Grey-blue against the twig-tips, thin air.

It is a beauty none but autumn has,
These drifts of blue-grey birds whom Nature binds
Into communities of single minds,
From early leaf-fall until Candlemas.

So in the failing Life when Death and Dread,
With axe and mongrel, stalk the withering wood,

The pigeons of the spirit's solitude
Clatter to glory at the stealthy tread,

And each, made deathless by the Spirit's joy,
Launch from the leaves that have forgotten green,
And from the valley seek another scene,
That Dread can darken not, nor Death destroy.

Autumn Ploughing

After the ranks of stubble have lain bare,
And field mice and the finches' beaks have found
The last spilled seed corn left upon the ground;
And no more swallows miracle in air;

When the green tuft no longer hides the hare,
And dropping starling flights at evening come;
When birds, except the robin, have gone dumb,
And leaves are rustling downwards everywhere;

Then, out, with the great horses, come the ploughs,
And all day long the slow procession goes,
Darkening the stubble fields with broadening strips.

Gray sea-gulls settle after to carouse:
Harvest prepares upon the harvest's close,
Before the blackbird pecks the scarlet hips.

The Waggon-Maker

I have made tales in verse, but this man made
Waggons of elm to last a hundred years;
The blacksmith forged the rims and iron gears,
His was the magic that the wood obeyed.

Each deft device that country wisdom bade,
Or farmers' practice needed, he preserved.
He wrought the subtle contours, straight and curved
Only by eye, and instinct of the trade.

No weakness, no offence in any part,
It stood the strain in mired fields and roads
In all a century's struggle for its bread;
Bearing, perhaps, eight thousand heavy loads,
Beautiful always as a work of art,
Homing the bride, and harvest, and men dead.

November the Sixth

I face North-West upon a grassy hill,
Green ant-heaps under foot, behind me, briars,
With leaves like embers in decaying fires;
The sun is in blue sky, the clouds are still.

Over the valley facing me, a tump
Topped by a hawthorn bush, intensely shines;
A leafless wych-elm lifts her dainty lines,
A greenest ivy wreathes an oak-tree stump.

It is ten-forty, a November morning;
Two goldfinches upon the thistle kex
Cling to dig seed, a thrush is cracking snail,
Two pigeons pass, a rook caws between pecks;
The finches watch me as I watch the vale,
The owl within his yew-tree utters warning.

Pony Fair

Twice every year for full five centuries
This grass beside the road has held a fair,
Where horses have been sold from everywhere,
Each with some gloss of not-believed-in lies.
Here they have huddled close with frightened eyes,
Hearing the trumpets of the showmen blare,
Here they have cropped the roadside selvage bare,
And gone with their new masters down the rise.

Within the dream where horses run career,
(Being set free of men, when death at last
Slips halters off and knocks the shoes from feet),
How many must retread this quiet street,
Hoping to find some mistress of the past,
Or mother mare, or foal last looked on here.

Partridges

Here they lie mottled to the ground unseen,
This covey linked together from the nest.
The nosing pointers put them from their rest,
The wings whirr, the guns flash and all has been.

The lucky crumple to the clod, shot clean,
The wounded drop and hurry and lie close;
The sportsmen praise the pointer and his nose,
Until he scents the hiders and is keen.

Tumbled in bag with rabbits, pigeons, hares,
The crumpled corpses have forgotten all
The covey's joys of strong or gliding flight.

But when the planet lamps the coming night,
The few survivors seek those friends of theirs;
The twilight hears and darkness hears them call.

The Towerer

Old Jarge, Hal, Walter and I, the Rector and Bill,
The old red setter and Joe, the retriever, Bess,
Went out in the cider time for something to kill,
Past Arthur's Camp, a couple of miles, I guess.

We came in the noon of the blue September day
To a tongue of grass thrust into a cleft of copse,
Berries were black and plump on the changing spray,
A dwindled spring went over its lip in drops.

We stopped to drink at the spring, Hal, Walter and I,
The retriever, Bess, the old red setter and Joe.
A covey went up with a whirr and the guns let fly,
The birds went skimming the trees towards Barney's Low.

They fired two last long shots, the Rector and Bill,
A feather came out of a bird, but the bird went on.
"Hit him," they said; we muttered, "You didn't kill."
Over the tips of the trees the covey was gone.

The hit bird swerved from the line of the covey's charge,
Over the grass of the field we watched him rise:
"Got him," the Rector said. "Her towers," said Jarge.
We saw him breast like a lark the hot blue skies.

He climbed the air till he struggled in sky alone,
Straining and beating up on a battling breast,

84

Then paused, then dropped with a thump upon bounding
    bone:
Joe brought him in; we bagged him up with the rest.

At covey-call time in the dusk September eve,
We loitered home together and shared the kill:
Nine brace, three rabbits, a hare: we all took leave;
Jarge took the dogs: the moon came over the hill.

Poor Bess, the retriever, died, her muzzle all white;
A run-away cart ran over the spaniel, Joe;
Jarge died of a quart of rum next Christmas night;
The old red setter went west, oh, ages ago.

Bill died from shock of a fall, as his heart was weak,
The Rector lingered to die of a sheer old age;
Walter went down with a stroke and could not speak,
He, too, has gathered his goods and drawn his wage.

Only Hal and myself of the nine remain,
And Hal's forgotten the bird, forgotten the shoot,
The grass, the wood and the spring are here in my brain,
With the dogs and the wine-leaved brambles black with
    fruit.

I think of the towering bird with its choking lung,
Its bursting heart, its struggle to scale the sky,
And wonder when we shall all be tried and hung
For the blue September crime when we made it die.

Candlemas Day

The frost is passing; from the West the rain
Sets slowly in with valley mistings cold;
The rabbit shudders in his earthy hold,
The earth-worm wriggles towards love again.

The lambs are in the straw-fold, shivering,
The starlings on the roof discuss together,
But the blithe chaffinch, sure of sunny weather,
Utters his chatter till the copses ring.

The fox still cries by night, the geese still haunt
The mudlands waiting for the March's moon;
The year is waiting for the secret sign.

The last leaves of the bramble peak and pine,
The buds are firm, the snowdrop blossoms; soon
Blackbirds will sing and cuckoo-flowers flaunt.

The Eyes

I remember a tropic dawn before turn-to,
The ship becalmed, the east in glow, a dimness,
Dark still, of fleece clouds mottled to the zenith,
The seamen as men dead upon the deck,
Save three who watched, dark statues they, dark bronze.
All things were silent save uneasy gear,
So silent that one heard the flying fish
Startling in frisk and plopping in the sea,
So many that we knew that multitudes
Of living things were near us though unseen.

Marvellously the fleece clouds changed from dim
Through every lovely colour into gold,
And then through every light to intense gleam,
Until a miracle of burning eyes
Looked down upon our thirty distinct souls.

Each of us and the fishes in the deeps,
And every flitting sprite that leapt and sped,
Those watchers knew and called each by his name.

The Spanish Main

Low, dull-green hills with scrub and little trees,
A long, straight pier that widens to a wharf,
On which three lines of freight-cars bake in the sun,
And one tall travelling derrick stands up black.

At the pier-base, a beach and tiny town:
Two hundred little huts with reddish roofs,
Straggle along the selvage of the bay,
Thicker and higher nearer to the pier,
Scanter to eastward where the lighthouse stands,
A thin white finger near a river bridge.

Southward, the hills are higher, and the bay
Something like Anzac; on the beach a wreck
Blisters; to eastward lies another wreck,
Two masts and four old davits all burnt black,
With one limp wire guy not worth the salving.

Northward, a three-mile island like a pier
Hedges the bay: a league of surf is on it.
Beyond, appalling surf breaks on a cliff.
Two speedy little fish-boats sail for fish;
Each sets a big lateen and tiny jib,
The foot of the lateen topped high aloft
Upon a bending boom: they fly like birds.
An old man and a boy are in the nearest:
The old man steers and hauls a silver fish.

We discharge cases from the after hold;
Twelve negroes slowly load them in the cars;
They are superb men, dark as dark-brown horses,
They move with grace, bare-armed up to the shoulders.
They wear blue cotton trowsers and white singlets,
And very old, crushed, yellow straw sombreros.
They have such beauty in their supple strength;
They dance as they bear cases. On the pier,
Two pale brown men, in purple bathing-drawers,
Walk bare-foot and bare-headed in the sun.
They have been diving to inspect the piles
Crushed by our starboard broadside as we berthed.

More natives at the gangway offer wares:
Red moccasins, the polished horns of cows,
Grass-woven purses, boxes of split cane,
Stuffed baby alligators, rattles, gourds,
Blue wool-work slippers, and grey lucent shells,
And boxes of split straw that look like muslin.
They dust these jealously with cotton cloths.

Twin brothers with their arms about each other
Stand at the pier-end, staring at the ship.

Nombre de Dios

The jungle reaches to the water's edge.
Behind where once the city stood, a valley,
Doubtless a water course, slants inland westward
Between low hills; inland are higher hills,
How high I cannot see, the rain is on them
In swathes and fading smokings of gray cloud.
Close to the city site a gleam of sun
Lights up the dark green and the brighter green
Of jungle near the shore, and the surf shines.

Now, to the eastward of the bay, I see
What Drake and his companions called the Mount.
It is still levelled as the Spaniards left it,
But all grown green with jungle like the rest.
Drake, when he took the city, hurried there
To find if cannon had been mounted yet.

*　　　*　　　*

It is three hundred years since any cannon
Were fired here, or any city stood.
For half a lifetime I have longed to see
This port of old romance: it opens . . . see.

*　　　*　　　*

Slanting across the harbour mouth, a knoll,
Dark, almost black, just from a blacker hill

90

Like a dark finger pointing to the site;
A rock breaks water near the harbour entrance.

*   *   *

That gully in the coast is all it is,
The site of thirty houses built of wood,
A wooden church, two treasure barns of stone,
An earthwork, and an unsafe anchorage
Where ships would drag with seven anchors out.
Drake's blood was shed there and his heart was broken,
Drake burned it to the jungle that it is.

*   *   *

Yet, what a tribute to the strength of Spain,
The builders came by ship four thousand miles,
'Stablisht their paltry village and endured,
The steam, the heat, the thirst, the flies, the fever.
Then in their manhood hacked the jungle through,
Found the Pacific, builded ships and sailed
Onward, undaunted, to the unknown world.

Porto Bello

The port is unsuspected from the east,
Slowly the bay draws open, with still water,
Deeper and deeper yet, to the calm pond,
Hot, stagnant, wrinkleless, of palest gray.

There is the city at the end at last,
The dirty, gray stone platform of the fort,
To left of what remains, a few small houses,
The little river and a scarlet barn.

Once all the bells in England rang with joy
That we had captured this; we have two poems,
A painting and commemorative pots
(Jugs and quart mugs) which celebrate the feat.

Two generations since, an English ship
Lay here surveying: one aboard her told me
That all her seamen were beset with boils
Like Egypt in the Book of Exodus;
Their chart is still the sailor's guidance here.

How many English bones lie underneath
That stirless water, Drake's men; Morgan's men;
The buccaneers; all Admiral Hosier's men;
The men with Vernon; christened in the fonts
Of English churches, and now welded white

With shells, or waving scarlet with soft tendrils,
Part of a sea-floor where no anchors fall
Nor any shadow of an English ship.
Near, in the blueness of the haze, an island
Rises before us as we pass the port;
It is Escudo, where Sir Francis Drake
"Yielded his valiant spirit like a Christian."
Some say "His heart is buried there": perhaps.
His body lies beneath us somewhere here.
The surf breaks on the island as we pass.

Canal Zone

Among these hills, twelve generations since,
The skirt-of-fortune-plucker, Francis Drake,
Saw from the watch-tree with the Indian prince
The bright Pacific basking like a snake.

Eastward and Westward lay the scenes achieved,
Southward, the deed to do, to Northward, foam
Lapsed on the grave, that waited, as it heaved,
The guest with darings done, not going home.

Now, new adventures hold. Across the track
Where once he stopped the treasure-mules, a 'plane
Roars to the air-base, bringing tourists back;
The spill-way thunders from the inland sea;
But quiet are the bonnet and the bee:
The Dragon slumbers beside sleeping Spain.

The Spanish Main Schooner

A little wooden schooner, painted white,
Lofty and beamy, likely to be fast,
Lies at the wharf beside the papaw sellers.
She has white wooden after-rails raised high,
A well-steeved bowsprit and a flaring sheer.

She has a deck-house just abaft the mainmast,
It brings the main-boom high above the deck,
The door is open, there are bunks within,
And yellow trousers dangling from a peg.

Outside it, on a box, a shining tin
Of soapy water holds the Captain's shirt.
A cock and hen find pickings on the deck,
Awnings of worn-out sail keep out the sun.

Her gear is white manila, nearly new.
All is in choicest order, the mast-shrouds
Are set-up by a method new to me.
The shrouds turn-in on double purchase-blocks,
The laniards reeve through dead-eyes on the rail.
The masts are raked, each little thing aloft
Is cared for with unusual seamanship.

Her seamen are on deck, four graceful negroes
Wearing white cotton clothing patched with blue,
Their arms are sunburned black up to the shoulder.

They stand below the mainmast, swaying up
Her mainsail white with cotton, the gaff jolts,
The mainsail ripples out, the negroes cry
Ahi, Aho. Upon her transom-stern
In white, on a green oval, is her name,
The SALVADOR DEL MUNDO. Cartagena.

A Ballad of Sir Francis Drake

Before Sir Francis put to sea,
He told his love, "My dear,
When I am gone, you wait for me,
Though you wait for seven year."

His love, who was redder than the rose,
And sweeter than the may,
Said, "I will wait till summer snows
And winter fields bear hay.

"I'll wait until the ice is hot,
And July sun is cold,
Until the cliffs of Dover rot,
And the cliffs of Devon mould."

Sir Francis went aboard his ship,
Her sails were sheeted home,
The water gurgled at her lip
And whitened into foam.

And months went by, but no more word
Came from that roving soul
Than comes from the Mother Carey bird
That nests at the South Pole.

In the seventh year men gave up hope,
And swore that he was dead.

They had the bell tolled with the rope
And the burial service read.

His love, who was redder than the rose,
Mourned for him long and long,
But even grief for a lover goes
When life is running strong.

And many a man beset her way
Who thought it Paradise
To gaze at her lovely eyes and say
That her eyes were stars, not eyes.

And so she promised a nobleman
When the ninth-year hay was hauled,
And before the harvest-home began
Her marriage banns were called.

The wedding-day came bright and fair,
The bells rang up and down,
The bridesmaids in their white were there
And the parson in his gown.

The rosy bride came up the aisle,
The page-boys bore her train;
She stood by the groom a little while
To be made one out of twain.

Not one of all within the church
Thought of Sir Francis Drake.
A crash made the transept columns lurch
And the central tower quake.

A cannon-ball came thundering by
Between the bride and groom.
The girl said, "Francis wonders why
There's someone in his room.

"Francis is homing from the seas,
He has sent this message here.
I would rather be wife to Francis, please,
Than the lady of a peer."

Ere the priest could start his talk again,
A man rushed in to say,
"Here is Drake come home with the wealth of Spain.
His ships are in the Bay."

The noble said with courtly grace,
"It would be a wiser plan
If I let Sir Francis take my place,
And I will be Best Man."

The *Mayblossom*

(Told me by the Pilot)

The ship, *Mayblossom,* left Magellan Straits
And beat into a roaring Northerly.

Slowly she thrust into the strength against her;
The screw raced, the ship trembled, the plates groaned.
Up on her bridge, her Captain and two Mates
Saw in the blindness the Evangelists,
The four great rocks forever standing guard,
All wind-shrieked, sea-swept.

Slowly she beat to westward from the rocks,
Streamed, and turned northward for her Chilean port,
A half-league, then a league, upon her course;
Then, suddenly, the ship's propeller jarred
Off from its shaft and left her helpless there.

She drifted back; the Captain called all hands.
"Men, the propeller's gone; the ship is helpless.
We shall be on the rocks within the hour.
Any of you who choose may take the boats:
I shall stay by her and go down with her."

Half the ship's people chose to risk the boats.
One boat was smashed to pieces as she lowered.

The other, full of men, got clear away
And with a rag of sail beat from the ship
And no man ever heard of her again.
Meanwhile, the *Mayblossom*
Drifted upon the Four Evangelists;
The wind-shrieked, sea-swept.

Then, as she stumbled in the breakers' backwash,
When the great rocks hung up above the bridge,
And cataracts of billow fell back blind,
And all her fabric trembled from the blows
Of water thwarted by the basalt's face,
A wayward waif of current plucked her clear
And swept her South,
Towards the Horn,
To gray seas running forlorn,
Where ships are sown for corn,
And birds have screams in the mouth.

Having a Life and Hope and half a crew,
Captain and Engineer advised together,
Behind the dodger, as she rode the sea.
The Captain said,
"We've forty tons of gunny-sack, in bales,
Down in the forward hold: we might make sails
With that, if we had needles and some twine.
You have no twine or needles, I suppose?"
The Engineer replied, "We used to use them;

And always, still, when I indent for stores,
I ask to have a hank of twine and needle.
There should be one of each: I'll go to see."
Soon he came running back with shining eyes.
"Captain, a miracle has happened here:—
I wrote 'One hank of twine and one sail-needle' . . .
(Things which I never use, one trip in ten),
But by some miracle the chandlers sent
A gross of twine and gross of sail-needles.
See here, assorted sizes, England's best."
"You cannot beat the good God," said the Captain,
"For when He gives, He gives beyond all hope.
Now, when we've made some palms, we'll buckle-to,
And fashion sails and pluck her out of this."

They stitched a suit of sails: they contrived yards
From derricks, oars and handspikes: they set sail,
Ran eastward round the Horn and made the Falklands.

There, when the ship-repairers quoted terms,
The Captain told them, "Rather than pay that,
I'll sail her to the Mainland, and try there."

So said, so done: he sailed her to the Plate;
Shipped a propeller at a fairer price,
Then, under steam
Trudged the cold blackness of Magellan's stream
To that green water by a Chilean slip
That waited for the shadow of his ship.

1176 Hours

Oh, ticking Time, when wilt thou pass?
A thousand never-ending hours
Before the HAS TO BE is WAS
And all the desert IS is flowers.

Courage, the war passed that was long,
The other endless time went by;
This seven weeks would seem a song
From Heaven to men doomed to die.

Begone

Begone you rubbish of old dates
Of victims and the brutes who bleed 'em;
The intellectual beauty waits
An energy to give her freedom.

For underneath the seals of cells,
Waiting the rupture of endeavour,
The undiscovered wisdom dwells,
Whose freedom will be peace forever.

The Boy from Pauntley

West, in the redlands, good for hops and corn,
The famous Richard Whittington was born;
Thence, when his parents died, the little lad
Set off for London bearing all he had,
A kitten and a bundle of small gear.

He trudged the lambless Cotswolds, wintry-drear,
Saw Lechlade's shadows in the floods of Thames,
Dared the wind-haunted downlands with no names,
Then trod the beechlands to the flats beneath.
But ever in his heart, by hill or heath,
The comfort burned, that soon he would behold
London, the city ever paved with gold.

Before the friendless Cotswold miles were done
The silver pennies in his purse were gone.
In Berkshire, shirt by shirt, he stripped his pack,
At Henley, sold the jacket from his back,
At Maidenhead, the shoes upon his feet,
For shelter from the storm and food to eat.
When at cold Candlemas he entered in
At London's Ludgate, looking for an inn,
His kitten was his only wealth unspent.

Hopeful, at first, as children are, he went
Knocking at doors, hope growing ever dim
That men might pity childhood if not him.

Alas, he found no pity anywhere.
Who pities hungry children with feet bare?
Are they not little devils, thieves or worse?
"Get out, you little scoundrel, with God's curse.
Let me but catch you here again, my son,
And you'll repent it," so said everyone.
Friendless as no-one but a child can be
He trod the alleys in his misery,
Feeling the pangs which none but children know
Whose spirits shrivel at the brand of woe;
Groping among the gutters for the scraps,
Crust for himself and herring-heads perhaps
For his beloved cat, the last link left
Of happy days before he was bereft;
Sleeping at night, (or drowsing, shivery-sick),
On some church porch's flagging, huddled thick
With wretches like himself, for whom Christ died.

It chanced, Dick and his kitten were espied
By William Grocer, trading in Cheapside,
Who for the moment lacked a boy to sweep,
Run errands, and fetch parcels, for his keep,
"To train in industry," as William phrased
Working and starving children until dazed.
    William the Grocer called his wife to door:—

MR. GROCER: "See, dear, the little boy who came before
    Asking for work and looking hunger-bitten,
    The little white-faced urchin with the kitten."

Mrs. Grocer: "Well, and what of it? I've my work to
  do."
Mr. Grocer: "Why, it occurs, he might be helping you."
Mrs. Grocer: "That little scarecrow without even shoes.
  His feet all filthy from the gutter ooze?
  Who knows what den he comes from, or what
    thieves?"
Mr. Grocer: "Yes, but tonight, remember, Simkin leaves.
  We have not found a boy to take his place.
  The child has marks of breeding in his face."
Mrs. Grocer: "Yes, gallows-breeding: orphaned last
  assize."
Mr. Grocer: "One must not judge a servant till one tries.
  Let's give him trial: if we wash him sweet,
  Simkin's shoes (stuffed) would go upon his feet,
  And Simkin's coat would fit him, with a tuck
  Put in the sleeves and elsewhere, with good luck.
  He would not need much food, and as for bed,
  The child could sleep as soundly as the dead
  Down in the cellar, upon packing straw.
  We should not pay him: for it is God's law
  Never to pamper licence in the young."
Mrs. Grocer: "To me, he looks as if he would be hung.
  But still, I don't mind trying: he'll soon see
  What he will get from running foul of me.
  See that he washes in the trough without,
  Ere coming in; he's pretty foul, I doubt."

William the Grocer called the little boy.

Mr. Grocer: "Child, I can offer you a good employ,
Lodging and board and honest clothes to wear,
(Better than living broke and going bare).
I cannot give you money: only keep,
Good food, warm raiment and a place to sleep.
As for your petted kitten, he can stay
Down in the cellar to keep mice away."

To little Dick, the grocer's offer seemed
The very being of a Heaven dreamed.
He vowed to show his thanks by toiling hard.

Thenceforward, before dawn, he swept the yard,
Mopped-out the shop and scrubbed the doorstep
    clean,
Raked out the ashes where the fire had been,
Laid and blew up the fire and prepared
The breakfast for the grocer, ever scared
Less Mistress should accuse him of the theft
Of some old crust or skin of sausage left.
Then, having served the breakfast, sick with fear
Of Mrs. Grocer's fist across his ear,
He washed the dishes and was free to eat
Such leavings as the dragoness thought meet.
Then, when the shop was opened, he became
Drudge for the day to dragon and to dame,
Fetching from cellar, lifting from the shelf

Boxes and cases bigger than himself,
Packing the purchases and ever curst
If cases fell, goods spilled or package burst.
Then with a hand-cart and with nerves a-quiver,
He hurried forth with parcels to deliver,
This to be there by ten, and that delayed,
And t'other kept unless the bill were paid.

Delivering these was daily martyrdom
From fear of snatch-thieves grabbing goods or pay.
When he returned to scoldings for delay,
There were still errands to be run, or cases
To drag from cellar or return to places.
Now cursed for slowness by his lord, now getting
Boxes on ears from Mistress for forgetting,
He hurried as a drudge to blow or blame
Till shopping time was passed and darkness came.

Then, when the shop was shut and sweeping done,
And all the shelves made tidy every one,
And all unmarketable dainties rolled
With marketable, that they might be sold;
When supper had been cooked and served and
        cleared,
And nightly curses given, nightly feared,
Then he could creep to find his cellar bed
And feed his cat before himself was fed,
And love his cat, remembering happy days

Riding the redlands on the Pauntley ways,
Watching the pigeons on the church roof ridge,
Or bright blue 'fishers flashing by the bridge.
Often when grocer had put out the light
He lay unsleeping, sobbing in the night,
While Puss with cold nose pushed or loud throat
    purred,
And St. Paul's belfry spoke his midnight word.

So five months passed, when, lo, there thither strayed
A great Sea Captain making up his trade
For some new voyage to the Ivory Shore.
The grocer and his wife, as once before,
Ventured their savings in the Captain's care
To purchase spice; and Dick and cat being there,
The Captain said, "What will you venture, son?"
Dick said, "Not money, sir, because I've none."
"No," said the grocer's wife, "nor that nor aught,
Save devil's gifts for making me distraught.
He and his cat are one continual wear."
"I like the lad; he has a lucky air,"
The Captain said, "Boys ought not to be good.
Boy, you shall venture with me, by the rood.
Give me your cat to trade with."
DICK: "O, sir, no.
She is my pet, I couldn't let her go."
CAPTAIN: "Nonsense, my cockrel, hand her over here."

The Dragoness took Richard by the ear:

MRS. GROCER: "O, so you couldn't and you wouldn't
        neither?
    Nothing will break your stubborn heart but leather.
    What? When the Captain offers, you refuse?
    I'd make your little body all one bruise
    If I'd my way, refusing him like that."
THE CAPTAIN: "Ah, Mistress, no; he'll let me have the cat.
    Come, Pussy, come: she'll bring you all the trade
    A cat may bring; so give her." Dick obeyed.

    So Puss was handed over and a dart
    Of very sorrow panged in Richard's heart.
    Puss, who had known the happy days of old
    Before the strangers came and home was sold,
    Puss, who must still remember sleeping soft
    Under the roof-ridge of the pigeon-loft,
    Puss to be gone abroad was bitter pain.
    "See how he sells his Mother's cat for gain,"
    The Dragoness said, sneering; "but, alas,
    Children have no more feeling than this brass."

THE CAPTAIN: "To sea, then, Pussy; we must catch the
        tide."

    Dick watched the vessel leave the river side,
    Hoist sail and slowly dwindle and grow dim,
    And now his only friend was gone from him.
    She was away, and he had none for friend
    Thenceforward after dark at cellar-end.

III

Thenceforward, Richard's life grew daily worse;
Daily his Mistress would abuse and curse;
Daily his Master dealt him strap or stick
For being right or wrong or slow or quick,
Till, at the last, his cup of woe was filled.

Then, since his utmost seemed not what they willed.
He planned to run away and seek new life,
Far from the poison of this man and wife,
Far from the cellar where the death-watch struck
Nightly all night his signal of ill-luck;
Far from the hell where all he had to give
Brought but the curse of only leave to live.

So, when the bells struck one he rose from bed,
And crept into the shop with tip-toe tread,
Then, stealthily removed the bell that hung
On the front door, that tinkled and gave tongue,
If any opened . . . Not a tinkle stirred.
Then the great key, in turning round, did gird,
Griding within the wheel box till it clocked.
His beating heart upon his rib-bones knocked,
Thinking the noise must rouse the grocer's wife,
Yet all was still. Then, trembling for his life,
He pulled the heavy door-bolts one by one.
They slid back to the guard, his task was done.
He moved the latch and held the door ajar.
Over the roofs he saw the Morning Star.

Along Cheapside a watchman with a bell
Moved on his beat and called that all was well.
The pigeons in the eaves stirred as he passed.

Then Dick slipped out and closed the door and cast
One hasty glance to see that no-one spied,
Then fled into the world, which opened wide
In dimness in a summer night just ending.

All still it was, save for the tom-cats wending
Home from their midnight jaunts to morning bed.
From ovens came the fragrant smell of bread
As bakers drew their loaves: a rambling din
Told where the market carts were loitering in.
Under the lantern at the gate, a cart
Already emptied lingered in its start,
The while the carter beat a linch-pin home.
"Bound for the North, young Master? Jump in . . .
    Come . . ."
The carter said, and led his horses through.
Dick from the waggon saw the fields in dew.
Watched by the dark-cloakèd sentries of the trees.
The hedges were all starred with dog-roses.

Soon, looking back, he saw the spires rise
Clean-cut against the dew-washed summer skies,
And thought that in those multitudes of men
None wanted him nor cared for him, and then,

Filled with his loneliness and misery
And hopeless future, he began to cry.

"Here," said the carter, "I must turn to load."
He helped Dick down, and left him on the road.

Upon the Roman Stone on Highgate Hill
Dick sat to look his last and weep his fill,
And as he wept and looked, the city chimes
Rang gently in his ears with ringing rhymes,
Each bell a voice that spoke into his brain.
"Turn, my Lord Mayor, Richard, turn again.
Turn into Guildhall out of Sorrow Lane.
Turn, Whittington: Turn, Whittington,
Three times Lord Mayor of London Town.

"Turn again, Whittington, Lord Mayor of London
    Town.
Turn again, Whittington, Lord Mayor of London
    Town.
Of London Town,
The great Lord Mayor;
From Sorrow Lane,
Yet thrice Lord Mayor."

"I am called back," he said. "They call me back . . .
And, if I go, I shall be thrashed, alack,
For going without leave; but I must go,
For luck will come, the bells have told me so."

And, hurrying back, ere he had gone a mile,
A passing carter let him ride awhile
Upon his waggon coming in with hay;
Then, nearer to the gates, a milkman's dray
Took him within the city to Cheapside.

He reached the grocer's house and no-one spied,
No-one was down, his going was not known.
He did his sweeping, trembling to the bone.
He cleaned the glass and made the shop all fair.
Then cheering sounded from the Water Stair.
Almost at once, with trumpets and with din,
A tumult from the Stairs came pouring in.
There, with a twelve months' beard and sea-wind's
    tan,
The Captain came, the tough sea-faring man,
Cheered by a crowd, and bearing on his shoulder
In cedarn crate, Dick's cat, a twelve month older.

"This is the house: descend, O cat of pride.
Come out, you grocer man," the Captain cried.
"Here, Steward, give the grocer man his spice:
Three sacks of nutmeg, fragrant beyond price,
Two bales of cinnamon, and all the rest.
Of all my ventures this has been the best.
Give me a chair and fill me in a drink.
Grocer, your wife grows lovelier, I think.
Mistress, to you, a long life, full of joy.

"But where's that jolly lad, the little boy?
The boy called Dick, that had the lucky look?
That ventured forth the pretty cat I took?
Ha, Dick, my son, come hither, lad, take hold.
This is your first-fruits, boy; a purse of gold.
But, Lord, I cannot talk: my wits are dulled:
Fetch up some wine and let us have it mulled:
Claret or porto, or whate'er it be,
All wine is wet on coming home from sea.

"Now that I've drunken I can tell the news.

"Friend Dick and Grocer, I have had a cruise
More prosperous than any ever made.
But yet of all the things I took for trade
My little Richard's cat succeeded most.
Here she returns, with nine lives, each with ghost.

"You should have seen the trouble on the Coast:
The savage King, with all his hundred wives,
Living in tree-tops, trembling for their lives,
Scared out of senses by a plague of mice.
"This Richard's cat, this Beast of Paradise,
During our voyage south had kittened seven.
Lord, when she came, she was a cat from Heaven.
She and her kittens cleared the mice from Court,
As quick as this sea-captain drinks this port.

"Glad? Why the King and Queens were so relieved
At being saved, it would not be believed.
They could not give enough to shew their thanks:
Ingots of gold and strings of pearls in hanks,
Ivory tusks and spice and silver bars,
And diamonds that shine as bright as stars,
All for this lucky Dick who sent the cat.
Come, Mistress Grocer, shew your joy hereat.
And Richard, come to wharf while we unlade.
The good Lord Mayor waits to see you paid."

So, as the bells had told, Dick's fortune turned.
He traded with his wealth and swiftly earned
A hundred times as much in ventures wise.
Merchant he was in all that money buys,
All that the sea can carry or land grow.
He was Lord Mayor thrice, he prospered so.

He founded three great hospitals and built
Guildhall anew and had its spires gilt.
King Richard knighted him, and when he died
The grateful city buried him in pride
Within the Abbey in a marble tomb.
There in the coloured lights and holy gloom
They show his scutcheon, seven cats' heads tabby,
Carved by the master mason of the Abbey.

Sweet Friends

Print not my life nor letters; put them by:
When I am dead let memory of me die.
Blessed be those who in their mercy heed
This heartfelt prayer of mine to Adam's Seed;
Blessed be they, but may a curse pursue
All who reject this living prayer, and do.